The CONFIRMATION BOOK

A Redemptorist Publication

Contents

Confirmation within Mass	3
Confirmation outside Mass	9
Confirmation Masses	10
Hymns	13

The CONFIRMATION BOOK
Published by:
Redemptorist Publications
Alphonsus House Chawton Alton Hampshire GU34 3HQ.
Copyright © The Congregation of the Most Holy Redeemer.
A Registered Charity

Eigth printing   September 1996 (88th thousand)

All rights reserved. No part of this publication may be reproduced, stored in a retrieval system, or transmitted in any form or by any means, electronic, mechanical, photocopying, recording or otherwise, without prior permission in writing from Redemptorist Publications.

English translation of the Rite of Confirmation.
Copyright © 1973, 1975 International Committee on English in the Liturgy, Inc.

Translation approved by the Bishops' Conference of England and Wales and Confirmed by the Sacred Congregation for the Sacraments and Divine Worship on 2nd February 1976 (Prot. n. 134/76)

      Concordat cum originali,
      Fr John Dewis
      3rd May 1976

ISBN 0 85231 161 3

Printed by Knight & Willson Limited Leeds LS11 5SF

Confirmation within Mass

The Mass may be that of the day or, except at certain seasons of the year, one of the special Masses on pages 10-12. The readings may be from the Mass of the day or from the special section for Confirmation in the Lectionary.

Homily

After the Gospel, those to be confirmed are called forward to the sanctuary, and the bishop gives a brief HOMILY in these or similar words:

On the day of Pentecost the apostles received the Holy Spirit as the Lord had promised. They also received the power of giving the Holy Spirit to others and so completing the work of baptism. This we read in the Acts of the Apostles. When Saint Paul placed his hands on those who had been baptized, the Holy Spirit came upon them, and they began to speak in other languages and in prophetic words.

Bishops are successors of the apostles and have this power of giving the Holy Spirit to the baptized, either personally or through the priests they appoint.

In our day the coming of the Holy Spirit in Confirmation is no longer marked by the gift of tongues, but we know his coming by faith. He fills our hearts with the love of God, brings us together in one faith but in different vocations, and works within us to make the Church one and holy.

The gift of the Holy Spirit which you are to receive will be a spiritual sign and seal to make you more like Christ and more perfect members of his Church. At his baptism by John, Christ himself was anointed by the Spirit and sent out on his public ministry to set the world on fire.

You have already been baptised into Christ and now you will receive the power of his Spirit and the sign of the cross on your forehead. You must be witnesses before all the world to his suffering, death and resurrection; your way of life should at all times reflect the goodness of Christ. Christ gives varied gifts to his Church, and the Spirit distributes them among the members of Christ's body to build up the holy people of God in unity and love.

Be active members of the Church, alive in Jesus Christ. Under the guidance of the Holy Spirit give your lives completely in the service of all, as did Christ, who came not to be served but to serve.

So now, before you receive the Spirit, I ask you to renew the profession of faith you made in baptism or your parents and godparents made in union with the whole Church.

Renewal of Baptismal Promises

All stand, and the Bishop (B) questions the Confirmands (C), who all reply together.

> *B:* Do you reject Satan and all his works and all his empty promises?

> *C:* **I do.**

> *B:* Do you believe in God the Father almighty, creator of heaven and earth?

> *C:* **I do.**

> *B:* Do you believe in Jesus Christ, his only Son, our Lord,
> who was born of the Virgin Mary,
> was crucified, died and was buried,
> rose from the dead,
> and is now seated at the right hand of the Father?

> *C:* **I do.**

> *B*: Do you believe in the Holy Spirit,
> the Lord, the giver of life,
> who came upon the apostles at Pentecost
> and today is given to you sacramentally in confirmation?

> *C:* **I do.**

> *B:* Do you believe in the holy Catholic Church,
> the communion of saints, the forgiveness of sins,
> the resurrection of the body, and life everlasting?

> *C:* **I do.**

A HYMN expressing faith may now be sung. Or the bishop accepts the confirmands' profession by proclaiming the Church's faith in these or similar words:

> *B:* This is our faith. This is the faith of the Church.
> We are proud to profess it in Christ Jesus our Lord.

All the faithful assent by answering:

> *All:* **Amen.**

The Laying on of Hands

The concelebrating priests stand near the bishop. He faces the people and with hands joined, sings or says:

B: My dear friends:
in baptism God our Father gave the new birth of eternal life
to his chosen sons and daughters.
Let us pray to our Father
that he will pour out the Holy Spirit
to strengthen his sons and daughters with his gifts
and anoint them to be more like Christ the Son of God.

All pray in silence for a short time.

The bishop and the priests who will minister the sacrament with him lay hands upon all the candidates (by extending their hands over them). The bishop alone sings or says:

B: All-powerful God, Father of our Lord Jesus Christ,
by water and the Holy Spirit
you freed your sons and daughters from sin
and gave them new life.
Send your Holy Spirit upon them
to be their Helper and Guide.
Give them the spirit of wisdom and understanding,
the spirit of right judgement and courage,
the spirit of knowledge and reverence.
Fill them with the spirit of wonder and awe in your presence.
We ask this through Christ our Lord.

All: **Amen.**

The Anointing with Chrism

The deacon brings the chrism to the bishop. Each candidate goes to the bishop, or the bishop may go to the individual candidates. The one who presented the candidate places his right hand on the latter's shoulder and gives the candidate's name to the bishop; or the candidate may give his own name.

The bishop dips his right thumb in the chrism and makes the sign of the cross on the forehead of the one to be confirmed, as he says:

Bishop: N., be sealed with the Gift of the Holy Spirit.
Confirmand: **Amen**

Bishop: Peace be with you.
Confirmand: **And also with you.**

If priests assist the bishop in conferring the sacrament, all the vessels of chrism are brought to the bishop by the deacon or by other ministers. Each of the priests comes to the bishop, who gives him a vessel of chrism.

The candidates go to the bishop or to the priests, or the bishop and priests may go to the candidates. The anointing is done as described above.

During the anointing a suitable song may be sung. After the anointing the bishop and the priests wash their hands.

General Intercessions

The general intercessions follow, in this or a similar form determined by the competent authority.

B: My dear friends:
let us be one in prayer to God our Father
as we are one in the faith, hope, and love his Spirit gives.

The deacon or minister reads the invocations:

D/M: For these sons and daughters of God
confirmed by the gift of the Spirit,
that they give witness to Christ
by lives built on faith and love:
Lord, hear us.

All: **Lord, graciously hear us.**

D/M: For their parents and godparents
who led them in faith,
that by word and example they may always encourage them
to follow the way of Jesus Christ:
Lord, hear us.

All: **Lord, graciously hear us.**

D/M: For the holy Church of God,
in union with N. our pope, N. our bishop, and all the bishops,
that God, who gathers us together by the Holy Spirit,

may help us grow in unity of faith and love
until his Son returns in glory:
Lord, hear us.

All: **Lord, graciously hear us.**

D/M: For all people,
of every race and nation,
that they may acknowledge the one God as Father,
and together seek his kingdom,
which is peace and joy in the Holy Spirit:
Lord, hear us.

All: **Lord, graciously hear us.**

B: God our Father,
you sent your Holy Spirit upon the apostles,
and through them and their successors
you give the Spirit to your people.
May his work begun at Pentecost
continue to grow in the hearts of all who believe.
We ask this though Christ our Lord.

All: Amen.

Liturgy of the Eucharist

Mass continues with the Liturgy of the Eucharist.

Blessing or Prayer

At the end of Mass, in place of the usual blessing, either the following BLESSING or PRAYER OVER THE PEOPLE is used.

1. Blessing

B: God our Father
made you his children by water and the Holy Spirit:
may he bless you
and watch over you with his fatherly love.

All: **Amen**

B: Jesus Christ the Son of God
promised that the Spirit of truth
would be with his Church for ever:

may he bless you and give you courage
in professing the true faith.

All: **Amen**

B: The Holy Spirit
came down upon the disciples
and set their hearts on fire with love:
may he bless you,
keep you one in faith and love
and bring you to the joy of God's kingdom.

All: **Amen.**

B: May almighty God bless you,
the Father, and the Son, † and the Holy Spirit.

All: **Amen.**

2. Prayer over the People

The deacon or minister invites the people in words such as:

D/M: Bow your heads and pray for God's blessing.

B: God our Father,
complete the work you have begun
and keep the gifts of your Holy Spirit
active in the hearts of your people.
Make them ready to live his Gospel
and eager to do his will.
May they never be ashamed
to proclaim to all the world Christ crucified
living and reigning for ever and ever.

All: **Amen.**

B: And may the blessing of almighty God,
the Father, and the Son, † and the Holy Spirit,
come upon you and remain with you for ever.

All: **Amen.**

Confirmation outside Mass

A PSALM or HYMN (hymns pages 13-15) may be sung as the bishop and his ministers come to the altar.

The bishop greets the people:

> *B:* Peace be with you.
> *All:* **And also with you.**

> *B:* Let us pray.
>
> God of power and mercy,
> send your Holy Spirit to live in our hearts
> and make us temples of his glory.
> We ask this through our Lord Jesus Christ, your Son,
> who lives and reigns with you and the Holy Spirit,
> one God, for ever and ever.

> *All:* **Amen.**
>
> Or one of the prayers may be said from the Confirmation Masses (pages 10-12).

Celebration of the Word of God

The celebration of the Word of God follows. At least one of the readings suggested for the Mass of Confirmation is read.

Sacrament of Confirmation

The rite is as that during Mass, beginning with the HOMILY (page 3) At the end of the GENERAL INTERCESSIONS (page 7) the bishop introduces the OUR FATHER in these or similar words.

> *B:* Dear friends in Christ,
> let us pray together
> as the Lord Jesus Christ has taught us.

> *All:* **Our Father…**

Blessing or Prayer

The BLESSING or PRAYER OVER THE PEOPLE follows as given on pages 7 & 8.

9

Confirmation Masses

(not for use on Sundays of Advent, Lent or Easter, or other Solemnities, nor may they be said on Ash Wednesday or during Holy Week).

Mass No. 1

ENTRANCE ANTIPHON (Ezek. 36: 25-26)

I will pour clean water on you and I will give you a new heart, a new spirit within you, says the Lord.

OPENING PRAYER

1. God of power and mercy,
   send your Holy Spirit to live in our hearts
   and make us temples of his glory.
   We ask this through our Lord Jesus Christ, …

   or

2. Lord,
   fulfil your promise.
   Send your Holy Spirit to make us witnesses
      before the world
   to the good news proclaimed by Jesus Christ
      our Lord,
   who lives and reigns…

   or

3. Lord,
   fulfil the promise given by your Son
   and send the Holy Spirit
   to enlighten our minds
   and lead us to all truth.
   Grant this through our Lord Jesus Christ, …

   or

4. Lord,
   send us your Holy Spirit
   to help us walk in unity of faith
   and grow in the strength of his love
   to the full stature of Christ,
   who lives and reigns…

PRAYER OVER THE GIFTS

Lord,
we celebrate the memorial of our redemption
by which your Son won for us the gift of the Holy Spirit.
Accept our offerings,
and send us your Holy Spirit
to make us more like Christ
in bearing witness to the world.
We ask this through Christ our Lord.

HANC IGITUR

(for use with the EUCHARISTIC PRAYER I)

Father, accept this offering
from your whole family
and from those reborn in baptism
and confirmed by the coming of the Holy Spirit.
Protect them with your love and keep them close to you.
(Through Christ our Lord. Amen.)

COMMUNION ANTIPHON (cf. Heb. 6: 4)

All you who have been enlightened, who have experienced the gift of
heaven and who have received your share of the Holy Spirit: rejoice in
the Lord.

PRAYER AFTER COMMUNION

Lord,
help those you have anointed by your Spirit
and fed with the body and blood of your Son.
Support them through every trial
and by their works of love
build up the Church in holiness and joy.
Grant this through Christ our Lord.

Mass No. 2

ENTRANCE ANTIPHON (cf. Rom. 5: 5, 8: 11)

The love of God has been poured into our hearts by his Spirit living in
us.

OPENING PRAYER

Lord,
send us your Holy Spirit
to help us walk in unity of faith
and grow in the strength of his love
to the full stature of Christ,
who lives and reigns with you and the Holy Spirit,
one God, for ever and ever.

(Other prayers from Mass No. 1 may be chosen)

PRAYER OVER THE GIFTS

Lord,
you have signed our brothers and sisters
with the cross of your Son
and anointed them with the oil of salvation.
As they offer themselves with Christ,
continue to fill their hearts with your Spirit.
We ask this through Christ our Lord.

HANC IGITUR

(as Mass 1 for EUCHARISTIC PRAYER I)

COMMUNION ANTIPHON (Ps. 33: 6. 9)

Look up at him with gladness and smile; taste and see the goodness
of the Lord.

PRAYER AFTER COMMUNION

Lord,
you give your Son as food
to those you anoint with your Spirit.
Help them to fulfil your law
by living in freedom as your children.
May they live in holiness
and be your witnesses to the world.
We ask this through Christ our Lord.

Hymns

1. COME, HOLY GHOST,CREATOR, COME

Come, Holy Ghost, creator, come
From thy bright heavenly throne,
Come, take possession of our souls,
And make them all thine own.

Thou who art called the Paraclete,
Best gift of God above,
The living spring, the living fire,
Sweet unction and true love.

Thou who art sev'nfold in thy grace,
Finger of God's right hand;
His promise, teaching little ones
To speak and understand.

O guide our minds with thy blest light,
With love our hearts inflame;
And with thy strength, which ne'er decays,
Confirm our mortal frame.

Far from us drive our deadly foe;
True peace into us bring;
And through all perils lead us safe
Beneath thy sacred wing.

Through thee may we the Father know,
Through thee th' eternal Son,
And thee the Spirit of them both,
Thrice-blessed Three in One.

All glory to the Father be,
With his co-equal Son:
The same to thee, great Paraclete,
While endless ages run.

2. COME DOWN, O LOVE DIVINE

Come down, O love divine,
Seek thou this soul of mine,
And visit it with thine own ardour glowing;
O comforter, draw near,
Within my heart appear,
And kindle it, thy holy flame bestowing.

O let it freely burn,
Till earthly passions turn
To dust and ashes in its heat consuming;
And let thy glorious light
Shine ever on my sight,
And clothe me round, the while my path illuming.

Let holy charity
Mine outward vesture be,
And lowliness become mine inner clothing;
True lowliness of heart,
Which takes the humbler part,
And o'er its own short-comings weeps with loathing.

And so the yearning strong,
With which the soul will long,
Shall far outpass the power of human telling;
For none can guess its grace,
Till he become the place
Wherein the Holy Spirit makes his dwelling.

3. MY GOD, ACCEPT MY HEART THIS DAY

My God, accept my heart this day,
And make it wholly thine,
That I from thee no more may stray,
No more from thee decline.

Before the cross of him who died,
Behold, I prostrate fall;
Let every sin be crucified,
And Christ be all in all.

Anoint me with thy heavenly grace,
And seal me for thine own,
That I may see thy glorious face,
And worship at thy throne.

Let every thought, and work and word,
To thee be ever given,
Then life shall be thy service, Lord,
And death the gate of heaven.

All glory to the Father be,
All glory to the Son,
All glory, Holy Ghost, to thee
While endless ages run.

4. HOLY SPIRIT, LORD OF LIGHT

Holy Spirit, Lord of Light,
From the clear celestial height,
Thy pure beaming radiance give;
Come, thou Father of the poor,
Come with treasures which endure;
Come, though light of all that live!

Thou, of all consolers best,
Thou, the soul's delightsome guest,
Dost refreshing peace bestow:
Thou in toil art comfort sweet;
Pleasant coolness in the heat;
Solace in the midst of woe.

Light immortal, light divine,
Visit thou these hearts of thine,
And our inmost being fill:
If thou take thy grace away,
Nothing pure in man will stay;
All his good is turned to ill.

Heal our wounds, our strength renew;
On our dryness pour thy dew;
Wash the stains of guilt away;
Bend the stubborn heart and will;
Melt the frozen, warm the chill;
Guide the steps that go astray.

Thou, on those who evermore
Thee confess and thee adore,
In thy sevenfold gifts descend:
Give them comfort when they die;
Give them life with thee on high;
Give them joys that never end.

5. CREATOR SPIRIT, BY WHOSE AID

Creator Spirit, by whose aid
The world's foundations first were laid
Come, visit every pious mind;
Come, pour thy joys on human kind;
From sin and sorrow set us free,
And make thy temples worthy thee.

O source of uncreated light,
The Father's promised Paraclete,
Thrice holy Fount, thrice holy Fire,
Our hearts with heavenly love inspire;
Come, and thy sacred unction bring
To sanctify us while we sing.

Plenteous of grace, descend from high
Rich in thy sevenfold energy;
Make us eternal truths receive,
And practise all that we believe.
Give us thyself, that we may see
The Father and the Son by thee.

Immortal honour, endless fame,
Attend the almighty Father's name;
The Saviour Son be glorified,
Who for lost man's redemption died;
And equal adoration be,
Eternal Paraclete, to thee.